# HOW CAN I BE SURE?

## BOB PHILLIPS

**HARVEST HOUSE PUBLISHERS**
Eugene, OR 97402

Cover design by Terry Dugan Design, Minneapolis, Minnesota

**How Can I Be Sure**
Copyright © 1978, 1999 by Harvest House Publishers
Eugene, Oregon 97402

ISBN 0-7369-0038-1

**Printed in the United States of America.**

99 00 01 02 03 04 05 / DH / 10 9 8 7 6 5 4 3 2 1

# About the Author

- Former director of the Northwest Counseling Center and the Fresno Counseling Center

- Executive director of Hume Lake Christian Camps

- Graduate of Biola University, La Mirada, California

- Graduate of California State University, Fresno, with a Masters in Counseling

- Graduate work with Fuller Seminary and The United States International University in the field of counseling

- Graduate of Trinity Seminary, Newburg, Indiana, with a Ph.D. in Counseling

- Licensed marriage, family, and child counselor

- Author of over 60 books with sales totaling more than 5 million copies

- Popular speaker in family-life seminars, churches, and conferences

- Devoted Christian husband and father of two children and believes that his family ranks at the top of his system of priorities and values

# Acknowledgments

I would like to extend a personal word of thanks to the following individuals who took time out of their busy schedules, to read this manuscript and make comments and suggestions:

Dr. Vince Bloom, associate professor of speech communications at California State University, Fresno

Dr. Henry Brandt, counseling psychologist

Dr. Ray Brewer, professor of education at California State University, Fresno

Richard Dickenson, professor of psychology at El Camino College and licensed marriage, family and child counselor

Dr. Howard Hendricks, chairman of the Dept. of Christian Education, Dallas Theological Seminary

Dr. Tim LaHaye, founder and president of Family Life Seminars and author of numerous books

Dr. Jeanne O'Dell, clinical psychologist and licensed marriage, family and child counselor

Ken Poure, extension director for Hume Lake Christian Camps and director of Accent Crusades, Inc.

Dr. Earl Radmacher, president of Western Baptist Seminary, Portland, Oregon

Dr. Ray Stedman, pastor of the Peninsula Bible Church, Palo Alto and author of numerous books

Dr. Jay Stevans, associate pastor of Northwest Church, Fresno, California

Dr. Paul Sundstrom, professor of pastoral psychology, Western Baptist Seminary, Portland, Oregon

Rev. Rick Yohn, pastor of Evangelical Free Church of Fresno, California, and author of numerous books

To

Ken Poure—

*Man of God*

*Leader of men*

*Spiritual father in the faith*

*My best friend*

# Contents

# Introduction

I hurt!

No, I'm not feeling any physical pain, I hurt emotionally. My pain comes from the anguish and suffering I have shared listening to couples relate to me the despair, frustration, and sense of hopelessness they are experiencing in their marriages.

I am a counselor, so my job is to listen and to help. But I do more than listen, I suffer with these couples. Part of my anguish comes from the realization that many of the problems I hear could have been avoided. So many times I have thought, *If only I could have counseled with this couple before they were married.*

As a busy counselor, I found that I was not only becoming involved with more and more divorce cases, but also with more and more premarital counseling. As I became involved in premarital counseling, I discovered a different type of frustration. How many sessions should I spend with a couple? What material should we cover? How much is enough? How can we approach sensitive subjects?

Jonathan Swift said, "Necessity is the mother of invention." The need for tools to help build strong foundations for marriage coupled with my frustration in premarital counseling led to the creation of this premarriage inventory.

This inventory is not an answer book for marriage problems. Many of those types of books have already been written and are available. This inventory is a discussion guide to help couples open up important channels of communication; express their thoughts, desires, and feelings to each other; and enhance their growing relationship together.

Each person should have a personal copy in which to write his or her own responses. If you will honestly share with each other your thoughts and feelings with regard to the questions, your future marriage will begin on a strong, firm, and mutually satisfying foundation.

Married couples can also benefit from a review of the questions. Discussing your responses together will help improve your communication and clarify any misunderstandings that may exist. Your love for each other will be revived, restored, and reinforced.

It is my prayer that you will find help and encouragement in these pages for your marriage and that God will be glorified as a result.

Bob Phillips
Fresno, California

# Using This Book

## For Pastors and Counselors

This book is designed to be a helpful tool in your hands. Therefore, you may want to present copies to the couple you are counseling or have both parties purchase their own copy.

In premarital counseling, it will be helpful to have the couple fill out the first three chapters prior to the initial session. A lot of time can be lost in counseling when either party or both have not considered certain topics ahead of time. This is complicated even further if the couple is embarrassed with the presentation of material that they have not yet discussed together. This is especially true in the area of sexual or financial topics.

Many couples have no idea what is involved in premarital counseling. This inventory helps to eliminate some of the fear and frustration and will greatly enhance the quality of the counseling sessions. The inventory will also help to add consistency to your premarital counseling program. The couples should be encouraged to complete the various homework assignments and bring the inventory with them to each session.

In developing this inventory, I have suggested six counseling sessions prior to the wedding. Some pastors or counselors may find fewer sessions satisfactory, while others may wish to meet more often. As you use the premarriage inventory, you will find it adaptable to your particular style of counseling.

Obviously, not every question mentioned needs to be covered in the presence of the pastor or counselor. Six counseling sessions would not be enough to cover all the material in this inventory. Certain key questions may be covered, or the counseling session could revolve around problem questions that the couple encountered prior to meeting with the pastor or counselor. Use those questions that would be most beneficial to the couple you may be counseling.

Here is a suggested breakdown of the material for six counseling sessions.

# Prior to the first counseling session

—Assign chapters 1, 2, and 3 to be completed

Session 1
—Discuss material in chapters 1, 2, and 3
—Assign chapters 4 and 5 as homework for Session 2

Session 2
—Discuss material in chapters 4 and 5
—Assign chapter 6 as homework for Session 3

Session 3
—Discuss material in chapter 6
—Assign chapter 7 as homework for Session 4

Session 4
—Discuss material in chapter 7
—Assign chapter 8 as homework for Session 5

Session 5
—Discuss material in chapter 8
—Assign chapters 9 and 10 as homework for Session 6

Session 6
—Discuss material in chapters 9 and 10
—Tie together any loose ends.

## *Additional Resources*

Chapters 11, 12, 13, 14, and 15 have been included as additional resource material. These chapters may or may not be used according to the needs of the couple and the counseling time that is available.

I feel that I must say a word about the material in chapter 8, "Sexual Inventory." In this chapter I have been very frank. The questions may be too embarrassing for some pastors, counselors, or couples to discuss together. (I hope this isn't the case.) If the pastor or counselor does not feel comfortable in discussing some of these issues with the couple, may I suggest that he or she encourage the couple to discuss them together or with a doctor. These questions have been collected from counseling sessions with married couples, who have all expressed the wish that they had faced these issues prior to their marriage.

## For Teachers and Leaders

Teachers and leaders may wish to use this inventory as:

—A course outline for teaching marriage and family issues
—A source of communication questions for small groups in
 churches, homes, conferences or retreats

## For Couples Alone

This inventory can be used with great benefit by couples who do not have the opportunity of premarital counsel with a pastor or counselor. The couple may use this as a guide to discussion in order to increase their communication with and knowledge of each other.

Married couples will find it helpful as a means to strengthen their relationship. They may also want to give this premarriage inventory as a gift to engaged couples they know.

# 1 *Family Background*

"You're just like your mother!" "You act the same way your father does!" These common statements are heard time and time again. In many respects, we are a product of our environment because our family backgrounds do affect our lives.

The way our parents treated us many times affects the way we will treat our spouses. Family traditions or the lack of traditions will influence our future marriages. The social and financial status of our childhood years play an important part in our adult thinking.

How much do you know about the family background of your future marriage partner? Are there potential problem areas? It has been said that when you marry, you marry the family. How well do you know your future spouse's family? Are you accepted by them? How well do they know you?

Answer the following questions and then discuss them together. Your discussion may trigger other family background questions which will help you gain deeper insights into each other and your families.

1. How old were your parents when you were born?

   Father _____                    Mother _____

2. List your brothers and sisters in order of birth (include yourself):

   1.                                          Age

   2.                                          Age

   3.                                          Age

   4.                                          Age

   5.                                          Age

   6.                                          Age

3. Were your parents ever:

   ❑ Separated   ❑ Divorced   ❑ Widowed?

   How old were you at the time?

   My parents' divorce affected me by:




   Who raised you?
   ❑ Father     ❑ Mother     ❑ Other

4. My parents are still living:  ❑ Yes   ❑ No

5. My parents' occupations are:

   Father

   Mother

6. I would describe my parents' marriage as:

   ❏ Very happy
   ❏ Usually happy
   ❏ Middle-of-the-road
   ❏ Sometimes troubled
   ❏ Very poor

7. I feel the leader in my home was:

   ❏ Father    ❏ Mother    ❏ Neither
   ❏ They fought for leadership

8. Describe your relationship with your:

   | *Father* | *Mother* |
   |---|---|
   | ❏ Affectionate | ❏ Affectionate |
   | ❏ Accepted | ❏ Accepted |
   | ❏ Tolerated | ❏ Tolerated |
   | ❏ Rejected | ❏ Rejected |
   | ❏ Persecuted | ❏ Persecuted |
   | ❏ Other | ❏ Other |

9. Describe the discipline style of your:

   | *Father* | *Mother* |
   |---|---|
   | ❏ Domineering | ❏ Domineering |
   | ❏ Strict | ❏ Strict |
   | ❏ Firm but kindly | ❏ Firm but kindly |
   | ❏ Permissive | ❏ Permissive |
   | ❏ Indulgent | ❏ Indulgent |
   | ❏ Other | ❏ Other |

10. I would describe my childhood as:

    ❏ Very poor          ❏ Sometimes troubled
    ❏ Middle-of-the-road ❏ Usually happy
    ❏ Very happy         ❏ Other


11. My parents think my marriage will be:


12. My parents' opinions toward my fiancé are:


13. Regarding my marriage, the parents of my fiancé think that:


14. The type of relationship I have with the parents of my fiancé is:


15. I see the following potential trouble points with my in-laws:


16. When I encounter difficulties with my in-laws, I will:

17. I think the following traditions and family traits of my family will affect my marriage:

18. If I have to live in the same house with my in-laws for a period of time, I will:

19. When my in-laws give advice, I will:

20. I have the following questions about in-laws:

# *2*
# *Previous Marital History*

You may have been married before. If so, please answer these questions. If you have not been married before, skip these questions and go on to the next chapter.

Many times, the individuals involved in second marriages carry into their new relationship problems and expectations out of their previous marriage. For example, if you had difficulty in communicating with your mate in your first marriage, will this trend continue? Why should your new relationship be any different? How will it be different? What will you do differently?

Problem areas are easier to identify than expectations. In your first marriage your mate may have taken care of and babied you when you were sick. In your second marriage, your mate may not baby you when you are sick. How will you feel about this? How will your new mate know what your expectations are?

The following questions are not exhaustive but may be helpful in starting discussion on potential problems and expectations brought about by more than one marriage.

1. Date of my first marriage:

2. How old were you and your ex-spouse when you married?

   Myself                              My ex-spouse

3.  How did the first marriage terminate?

    ❏ Divorce        ❏ Annulment        ❏ Death

4.  My marriage lasted for                years.

5.  Did you have any children by your previous marriage?

    ❏ Yes            ❏ No

    Name                                          Age

    Name                                          Age

    Name                                          Age

    Name                                          Age

    Name                                          Age

6.  The strong points of this marriage were:

    A.

    B.

    C.

    D.

    E.

7.  The conflict areas of this marriage were:

    A.

    B.

    C.

D.

E.

8. I have the following expectations about my new marriage, brought about by my previous marriage:

If you have only had one previous marriage please skip these questions and go on to the next chapter.

1. Date of second marriage:

2. How old were you and your ex-spouse when you married?

Myself                          My spouse

3. How did the second marriage terminate?

❏ Divorce        ❏ Annulment        ❏ Death

4. My second marriage lasted                    years.

5. Did you have any children by this second marriage?

❏ Yes          ❏ No

Name                                        Age

Name                                        Age

Name                                        Age

Name                                  Age

Name                                  Age

6. The strong points of this marriage were:

    A.

    B.

    C.

    D.

    E.

7. The conflict areas of this marriage were:

    A.

    B.

    C.

    D.

    E.

8. I have the following expectations about my new marriage, brought about by my previous marriages:

# 3

# *Status of Present Relationship*

Would you buy a car without shopping around? Would you purchase a house by only looking at the outside? Would you choose a vocation without looking at its positive and negative aspects? In most of the important decisions we make, we usually shop around, weigh the advantages and disadvantages, and count the cost. However, when it comes to one of the most important decisions in life—marriage—few people really examine the relationship to see if it is based on a solid foundation. How compatible are you with you future marriage partner? Do you have the same goals, interests, and expectations? Can you see yourself living with that person for the rest of your life?

Answer the following questions and share together how each of you views your potential partner.

1. I have known my fiancé for:

2. I first met my fiancé at:

3.  Have you announced your engagement yet?

    ❏ Yes        ❏ No        ❏ Planning to on _____

    Have you set a date for the wedding?


4.  My fiancé and I see each other:

    ❏ Every day                 ❏ 1-2 days per week
    ❏ 3-4 days per week         ❏ 5-6 days per week
    ❏ Less than once a week, _____ times per month

5.  Have you ever been engaged to anyone else?

    ❏ No      ❏ Yes     How long ago? _____

6.  The strong points I see in my fiancé are:

    A.
    B.
    C.
    D.
    E.
    F.
    G.


7.  I want to get married because:



8.  My definition of love is:

9. My fiancé and I have the following interests in common:

10. I think a good sense of humor in marriage is important because:

11. I feel that my fiancé's manners are:

12. My fiancé irritates me most when:

13. I feel our relationship has been most successful in:

14. I have the following expectations for my fiancé (leader, good cook, gentle, provider, etc.):

    A.

    B.

    C.

    D.

E.

F.

G.

15. My fiancé has the following expectations for me:

A.

B.

C.

D.

E.

F.

G.

16. I am happiest in our relationship when:

17. In our relationship I hurt most when:

18. My fiancé and I differ about the following things:

A.

B.

C.

D.

E.

F.

19. The following are some of the goals I would like to work toward in our marriage:

A.

B.

C.

D.

E.

F.

20. I believe my friends have the following opinions about this marriage:

21. Please check any of the following items you feel could be a potential barrier to this marriage:

❏ Divorce

❏ Pregnancy

❏ Abortion

❏ Cultural differences

❏ Racial differences

❏ Intellectual differences

❏ Economic differences

❏ Age difference

❏ Young or early marriage

❏ Parental conflicts

❑ Sexual problems
❑ Homosexual background
❑ Physical handicaps
❑ Personality differences
❑ Drug or alcohol use

Explain each item you checked:

# *4*
# *Religious Background*

Most people want a church wedding rather than a civil ceremony. Have you ever wondered why? What is so special about a church wedding? Sometimes couples really want their marriages blessed by God while others want a church wedding simply because it is a tradition. How important are religious and spiritual values to a marriage relationship? Does the spiritual life of couples affect their marriages? Do the vows of commitment made before God and friends really mean anything?

Answer the following questions and share with one another your religious and spiritual convictions.

1.  My father's religious background is:



2.  How religious is your father?

    ❏ Very              ❏ Middle-of-the-road
    ❏ Not very          ❏ Not at all

3.  My mother's religious background is:

4. How religious is your mother?

   ❑ Very            ❑ Middle-of-the-road
   ❑ Not very        ❑ Not at all

5. My religious background is:

6. How important do you believe religious commitments are to your marriage?

7. Do you believe in God?

   ❑ Yes        ❑ No        ❑ Unsure

8. Do you pray?

   ❑ No        ❑ Once in a while        ❑ Very often

9. Do you read the Bible?

   ❑ No                    ❑ Occasionally
   ❑ Fairly regularly      ❑ Regularly

10. Do you and your fiancé read the Bible together?

    ❑ Yes                    ❑ No

    If yes, how often do you read together?

11. Do you and your fiancé pray together?

❏ Yes ❏ No

If yes, how often do you pray together?

12. I attend church services:

❏ Never ❏ Seldom ❏ Periodically
❏ Frequently ❏ Regularly

13. The church I attend is:

Are you a member? ❏ Yes ❏ No

14. What do you think it means to receive Christ as your Savior and Lord?

15. Have you ever personally received Christ as your Savior and Lord?

❏ Yes ❏ No ❏ Unsure

If yes, where?

When?

16. What do you think it means to be a "Spirit-filled" Christian?

17. Do you consider yourself to be a Spirit-filled Christian?

    ❏ Yes          ❏ No          ❏ Don't know

18. My most significant spiritual experience was:

19. My definition of a Christian marriage is:

20. I want a church wedding because:

21. A Christian marriage is important to me because:

22. Do you believe that it is important for you and your family to go to church?

    ❏ Yes          ❏ No          ❏ Unsure

    Explain:

23. We plan to go to _____ church after we are married.

24. My fiancé and I have the following religious differences:

25. My fiancé and I plan to work on our religious differences by:

26. To me, equality before God means:

27. I believe that spiritual leadership in the home is initiated by:

28. I think that the spiritual growth of my children is the responsibility of:

29. We are planning for the following type of family devotions:

30. What do you think the phrase "to marry in the Lord" means?

31. Read Ephesians 5:15–6:4; Colossians 3:21; 1 Timothy 5:8; 1 Peter 3:7. Make a list of the responsibilities of a Christian husband:

32. Read Ephesians 5:15–6:4; 1 Timothy 1:9-10; 3:11; 1 Peter 3:1-6. Make a list of the responsibilities of a Christian wife:

33. I think  Psalm 127:1 means:

34. To me the word submission in Ephesians 5:21,22 means:

35. Does only the wife submit?

    ❑ Yes          ❑ No          ❑ Uncertain

36. I feel a husband can submit in marriage by:

37. After reading Genesis 2:24, I feel the phrase "one flesh" means:

38. Read Deuteronomy 24:1-4; Malachi 2:11-16; Matthew 5:31,32; 19:3-12; Mark 10:2-12; Luke 16:18; and 1 Corinthians 7:10-15. After reading the above Scriptures, I feel God's attitude toward divorce is:

39. I have the following questions about spiritual matters:

# Children

In many premarital counseling programs the issue of child-rearing is not dealt with in great detail. This is usually because of a time factor and because most couples are more concerned with immediate issues such as finances, marriage plans, and the sexual side of marriage.

Some couples do not plan for children or use forms of birth control to choose when to have children. Others can't wait to have children. What are your thoughts? Do you feel you should have children right away or do you plan to get to know your marriage partner better before having children? How long should a couple wait?

The following questions are designed to help you formulate your thoughts and verbally set forth a plan for child-rearing. Share together your thinking in this important area of marriage.

1. Do you plan to have children?

   ❏ Yes        ❏ No        ❏ Undecided

2. How many children would you like to have?

3.  How long would you like to wait before having children?

4.  Should a couple wait until they can afford to have children?

    ❏ Yes          ❏ No          ❏ Undecided

5.  I feel that it is important for the father to be present at the birth of a child.

    ❏ Yes          ❏ No          ❏ Undecided

6.  If we cannot have children, my feelings about adoption are:

7.  What are your feelings if you would have only boys or only girls?

8.  How much should a husband participate in the care of a baby?

9. What are your feelings toward sharing equally in all of the activities of care and raising of children (feeding, changing diapers, late-night responsibilities, etc.)?

10. The names of children should be determined by:

11. The responsibility for the discipline of the children lies with:

    ❏ Husband          ❏ Wife          ❏ Both

12. I want my children to learn the following values, rules, and characteristics:

13. My parents used the following discipline with me:

14. I want to discipline my children in the following ways:

    Early years

    Middle years

    Teen years

15. Who should be responsible for assisting children with home-work?

    ❑ Husband          ❑ Wife          ❑ Both

16. My thoughts with regard to leaving children in daycare or with babysitters are:

# Children

17. Who is responsible for buying clothes for the children?

    ❏ Husband        ❏ Wife        ❏ Both

    Comments:

18. Who decides what gifts to buy for the children?

    ❏ Husband        ❏ Wife        ❏ Both

19. I feel that the place of pets in the home is:

20. I feel that favoritism of children in the home is:

21. What is your opinion about standing behind your mate's discipline of the children?

22. If you have children by a former marriage, what will you want their relationship to be with the new father/mother?

23. If you have children by a former marriage, who will discipline your children?

24. If you have children by a former marriage, do you foresee any problems with visiting rights of the divorced partner? Explain:

25. In discipline, how strict do you think parents should be?

26. I think the most important thing in child discipline is:

27. I think that praising children involves:

28. How much should parents sacrifice for their children?

29. What are your thoughts about parents caring more for the children than for each other?

30. I think children should have the following privileges:

Early years

Middle years

Teen years

31. What message do you think is conveyed in Psalm 127 and Psalm 128?

32. Read Proverbs 22:6; 22:15; 13:24; 23:13,14; 29:15; 19:18; 29:17; Hebrews 12:5-11; Proverbs 20:30; Ephesians 6:4. After reading these verses, I think God's attitude toward discipline is:

33. I think having children will teach me the following lessons:

34. I have the following questions concerning child-rearing:

# 6

# *Finances*

Every couple experiences some degree of conflict or frustration in the area of finances. Finances rank among the big three of marital problems. (The other two are communication and sex.) The vast majority of couples who go into divorce courts are head over heals in debt.

How do you handle finances? Are you a spender or a saver? Do you like to use charge cards? Do you have a budget? Robert J. Hastings said that "money management is not so much a technique as it is attitude. And when we talk about attitudes, we are dealing with emotions. Thus, money management is basically self-management or control of one's emotions. Unless one learns to control himself, he is no more likely to control his money than he is to discipline his habits, his time or his temper. Undisciplined money usually spells undisciplined persons."[1] Do you agree with Mr. Hastings?

Fill out the following questions and share with your fiancé your thoughts concerning finances.

1. My attitude about the wife working outside the home is:

---

1. Robert J. Hastings, *The "10-70-20" Formula for Wealth: From the Marriage Affair* (Wheaton, IL: Tyndale House Publishers, 1971), p. 363.

2. State your attitude about the wife working outside the home after the birth of children:

3. Are you going to pool financial resources (gifts, savings, and earnings)? How?

4. If you have been married before, do you have any reservations or do you feel that there will be any problems in pooling finances from the former marriage (gifts, properties, savings, investments, insurance, trust funds or wills, etc.)? Explain:

5. I foresee the following problems with the "my money, your money" feelings:

6. My attitude toward debt, credit cards, borrowing money, and buying on time is:

7. If we experience financial reverses (unemployment, debt, sickness, etc.), I plan to:

8. Who will handle the checkbook?

9. Who will pay the bills?

10. What is your plan for budgeting?

11. How generous are you?

12. What are your thoughts about giving (church, charities, etc.)?

13. What are your thoughts about saving money (savings accounts, investments, property, retirement)?

14. What are your thoughts about life insurance?

15. What are your thoughts about health insurance?

16. How do you feel about writing a will?

17. What are your thoughts about the possibility of someday being financially responsible for your in-laws?

18. How do you feel about your spouse holding extra or part-time jobs?

19. What financial aspects do you think are involved in entertaining guests in your home?

20. If we get into financial difficulties, I will:

21. I have the following questions about finances:

## Super Simple Budget

A "Super Simple Budget" has been included for those couples who do not have a system of budgeting finances. There are usually three problem areas in family finances.

First, most couples do not know what the total of their fixed monthly expenses are (line 5). Because of this they buy items and have no idea of where they are financially until they are out of funds. (Very few arguments occur over fixed monthly expenses. You pay the rent or you are out on your ear. You pay your gas and electricity or they are turned off—without any argument with your mate.)

The second problem area occurs when the couple has bills totaling more than their monthly controllable income (line 6). When this happens, the couple usually puts all of their controllable monies towards their bills. This eliminates any extra cash flow. With no cash flow the couple can become frustrated and hostile. They have no money for emergencies, entertainment, or medicine. The couple might be wise to set aside some money for emergencies that may arise.

The third problem area revolves around who pays the bills. If one mate is not aware of how their money is being spent there can be trouble. For those who pay the bills I suggest the following:

1. Pay the fixed monthly expenses (usually no argument).

2. Come to your mate with the total of the fixed monthly expenses and the total of miscellaneous expenses. Show him or her what needs to be paid and how much you have to pay with.

3. Ask your spouse which bills need to be paid first and how much should be put on each bill. Then pay the bills as you both agreed. Then, when your mate asks you why a certain bill has not been paid you can relate to them your discussion and that you paid the bills according to your agreement.

# Finances

## *The Super Simple Budget*

### *Income (monthly)*

1. Salary or wages—husband ("take-home" after deductions)   $
2. Salary or wages—wife ("take-home" after deductions)   $
3. Other income (only list regular monthly income)   $
4. **Total Cash**—("take-home" income per month)   $

### *Fixed Monthly Expenses*

A. Giving   $
B. House payment/rent   $
C. Gas & electricity   $
D. Water & garbage   $
E. Food & household items   $
P. Car payment   $
G. Gasoline & oil   $
H. Car insurance   $
I. Life insurance   $
J. Loans   $
K. Union dues   $
L. Phone   $
M.   $
N.   + $_____
5. **Total Fixed Expenses**   $

> **Giving**
> **Tithing**—usually 10 percent of all income.
> **Love Giving**—giving out of love and in response to the benefits received from the Lord.
> **Faith Giving**—a promise to give an amount beyond ordinary income.
> **Sacrifice Giving**—giving to the Lord something that I really needed and wanted.
>
> *Everyone must make up his own mind as to how much he should give* (2 Corinthians 9:7 TLB).

Total Cash (line 4)   $
Fixed Expenses (line 5)   - $_____

6. Total Flexible or
   Controllable Monies   $

**Miscellaneous Expenses**

| | | |
|---|---|---|
| A. | Doctor, dentist, drugs | $ |
| B. | Clothing | $ |
| C. | Gifts | $ |
| D. | Entertainment, recreation | $ |
| E. | Allowances | $ |
| F. | Education, lessons | $ |
| G. | Savings (some, place their savings in "Fixed Monthly Expenses") | $ |
| H. | Car maintenance | $ |
| I. | Charge accounts | $ |
| J. | Babysitting/daycare | $ |
| K. | Home improvements | $ |
| L. | Subscriptions | $ |
| M. | Appliances | $ |
| N. | Incidentals | + $ |
| | Total | $ |

| | | |
|---|---|---|
| Controllable Monies from Line 6 (p. 53) | | $ |
| Less Buffer or Emergency Monies | | - $ |
| | Total | $ |
| Less Miscellaneous Expense | | - $ |
| | **Total** | |

# 7

# *Communication*

Reuel Howe, a gifted communicator, feels that "dialogue is to love, what blood is to the body. When the flow of blood stops, the body dies. When dialogue stops, love dies and resentment and hate are born. But dialogue can restore a dead relationship. Indeed, this is the miracle of dialogue: it can bring relationship into being, and it can bring into being once again a relationship that has died."[1]

Marjorie Umphrey in her book *Getting to Know You* defines communication:

1. Communication is giving and receiving a message.

2. Communication is giving of oneself.

3. Communication is receiving part of someone else.

4. Communication is sharing ideas, feelings and moments with another person.

5. Communication is experiencing another human being.

6. Communication is the giving and receiving of an emotional stroke.

7. Communication is getting my needs met.

8. Communication is meeting another person's needs.

9. Communication is looking at and seeing what another person is saying.

---

1. Reuel L. Howe, *The Miracle of Dialogue* (New York: The Seabury Press, 1963), p. 3.

10. Communication is listening and hearing what others are saying.

11. Communication is my face and body talking.

12. Communication is using all my senses to recognize what the other's face and body and voice is saying.

13. Communication is putting myself in the other's place.

14. Communication is touching.

15. Communication is reaching out.

16. Communication is tenderness and caressing.

17. Communication is words on the printed page.

18. Communication is allowing someone else to intrude into your world of thoughts.

19. Communication is expression through the arts.

20. Communication is spiritual.[2]

How well are you communicating? How open are you with each other? Do you feel free enough for your future life partner to get to know the real you? Answer the following questions and explore with your fiancé your deeper thoughts and feelings.

1. I think a person can change their mate by:

---

2. Marjorie Umphrey, *Getting to Know You* (Harvest House Publishers, 1976), pp. 20-21.

2. When I am emotionally irritated or bothered, my tendency is to:

> ❏ Act out or come on strong
> ❏ Withdraw and go into quiet irritation
> ❏ Other

3. State your opinion about keeping each other informed regarding schedules and whereabouts:

4. What will you do if your companion continually refers to your faults?

5. List things you think you would talk about at mealtimes:

6. How much should you share with your partner about work and other interests?

7. I can become more aware of my mate's feelings by:

8. How much time should be devoted to leisure time activities?

9. How much time should be devoted to the family?

10. How much time should be devoted to friends?

11. When I find my mate remaining silent for a long period of time, I will:

12. To what extent do you think your mate should pursue his/her interests, activities, and sports?

13. When I find that my mate is not as affectionate as I would like, I will:

14. When my mate yells at me, I will:

15. I think I can lift the spirits of my mate when he/she is depressed or discouraged by:

16. If a major illness strikes your mate, how will you react?

17. When my mate does something that displeases me, I will:

18. You may love your mate, but what are your thoughts about him/her being your friend?

19. When my mate sulks, whines, or pouts, I will:

20. When I find that my mate is not listening to me, I will:

21. When my mate uses the phrases "you always," "you never," or "everytime," I will respond by:

22. What are your thoughts about sharing unpleasant things that happen during the day?

23. I think I can help develop my mate's self-image by:

24. In clarifying misunderstood statements, I will:

25. I think that my mate and I need to improve our communication in the following areas:

26. I think my mate would like to change the following qualities or behaviors in me:

27. I express love to my mate in the following ways:

28. What are your feelings about marriage counselors and pastors helping you solve personal and marital problems?

29. I have the following educational plans:

30. I have the following vocational plans:

31. I would like to ask the following questions about communication in marriage:

## More Communication Questions for Discussion

1. I think the best time of day to talk over marital difficulties is:

2. The types of things that get on my nerves are:

3. State your opinion about your partner talking about former sweethearts or a former spouse:

4. When my mate says one thing and means another, I will:

5. I can compliment and praise my spouse more by:

6. When my mate goes out often with the guys/gals, I feel:

7. What are your thoughts about telling jokes at your partner's expense?

8. What are your opinions about correcting your mate in public?

9.  I like to do the following activities with my mate:

10.  When I find it difficult to confide in my mate, I will:

11.  How can you help your mate when he/she is upset because of work, children, or some conflict with another person outside of your marriage? How much sympathy do you give? How much encouragement? How much correction?

12.  What is your opinion about discussing your spouse's faults in public?

13. What are your thoughts about nonverbal communication in marriage?

14. What are your thoughts about arguing in public?

15. It has been said that marriage is a 50–50 partnership. What do you think?

16. I am easily offended in the following ways:

17. What are your thoughts about discussing in-laws in public?

18. I think that personality clashes are caused by:

19. I think that jealousy and possessiveness are caused by:

20. How important do you think it is for a husband and wife to discuss intellectual and emotional issues such as race relations, politics, religion?

# *8*
# *Sexual Inventory*

Seldom does a week go by that I don't do some form of sexual counseling. I never cease to be amazed that, although we live in a sex-saturated culture, little good sex knowledge is known by the common man or woman on the street. I have had individuals in my office who stated that their families were very open in the discussion of sex. They also felt they were very knowledgeable in this area. Yet, as we talked further, I could see how little they knew and how embarrassed they were to talk on this subject.

The following questions are frank and deal with common problems encountered in giving sexual counsel. It has been my experience that most couples do not talk about sexual matters very deeply, even after they are married. These questions deal with real issues. A great deal of frustration, hurt, fear, and anger could be eliminated if these issues were faced by the couple *before* they became crisis points in what is designed by God to be a most beautiful experience.

I encourage you to discuss together the following questions.

1.  Have you had a physical examination for your marriage?

    ❏ Yes          ❏ No

2.  Do you have any health problems? Explain:

3.  Are you bringing any sexually transmitted diseases into this relationship?

4.  At this particular time, I think about sex:

    ❏ Seldom          ❏ Periodically
    ❏ Frequently      ❏ Regularly

5.  My present feelings about sex are:

    ❏ Disturbed    ❏ Fearful    ❏ Anxious    ❏ Neutral
    ❏ Expectant    ❏ Excited    ❏ Intrigued

6.  Do you have any sexual inhibitions, fears, or awkward feelings? Explain:

7.  What was your impression of your parents' sex life?

    ❏ Fulfilling    ❏ Warm    ❏ Casual    ❏ Neutral
    ❏ Tolerant      ❏ Cold    ❏ Empty

8. Were you the victim of any unpleasant sexual experiences as a child, adolescent, or adult?

   ❏ No          ❏ Incest        ❏ Raped
   ❏ Molested    ❏ Homosexual encounter
   ❏ Indecent exposure
   ❏ Other

9. Who do you think is responsible for birth control?

   ❏ Husband           ❏ Wife           ❏ Both

10. In planning to postpone or not having children, the form of birth control method I prefer is:

    ❏ Withdrawal      ❏ Rhythm        ❏ Douche       ❏ Foam
    ❏ Birth control pills ❏ Vasectomy  ❏ Contraceptive jelly
    ❏ Condom          ❏ Diaphragm     ❏ Cervical Cap
    ❏ Tubal ligation  ❏ Abortion      ❏ Hysterectomy
    ❏ IUD             ❏ Vaginal suppositories

11. Who do you think should initiate sexual activity?


    Why?




12. Who do you think should determine the way, the place, how often, length of time, and variety of sexual activity?

13. How do you feel about seeing you partner nude?


14. How do you feel about having your partner seeing you nude?


15. State your thoughts about the following:

Lip kissing


Tongue kissing


Your partner kissing your body


Kissing of your partner's body


Caressing your partner's body


Your partner caressing your body


Kissing your partner's genitals

Your partner kissing your genitals

Bringing your partner to a climax by hand

Your partner bringing you to a climax by hand

Bringing your partner to a climax by oral stimulation

Your partner bringing you to a climax by oral stimulation

16. How important do you think simultaneous orgasm is?

17. A woman reaches orgasm by:

18. Why is it important to communicate about sexual desires?

19. Why is it important to verbally tell your partner what stimulates you sexually?

20. What are your thoughts about intercourse during the woman's menstrual period?

21. What type of menstrual period do you or your fiancé have?

22. How many times per week do you think that you would like to have intercourse?

23. I think the act of intercourse should last:

24. I would prefer a lovemaking environment that includes (lighting, music, etc.):

25.  Privacy in lovemaking is important because:

26.  At what time of day should lovemaking take place?

27.  What are your thoughts as to where lovemaking should take place?

28.  What are your thoughts about various positions in intercourse?

29.  What will you do when the man has difficulty in maintaining an erection?

30.  What will you do when the man has difficulty with premature ejaculation?

31. What will you do when you find the woman cannot reach a climax?

32. What will you do when you find the woman cannot reach a climax with the penis inserted into the vagina?

33. How important do you think the act of intercourse is on the honeymoon night?

34. What will you do when the man cannot make entrance into the woman and complete the act of intercourse due to tightened vaginal muscles or pain in the vaginal area?

35. Suppose that you have been married for a period of time, and one day you discover your mate masturbating. What will you do?

36. What might you do if you find that your partner does not like the act of intercourse?

37. How do men and women differ in their readiness for sexual climax?

38. If I discovered my partner was romantically interested in another person, I would:

39. Why are things like kind words, gentle touches, and kind deeds important in the lovemaking process?

40. Do you think you will be able to refuse sexual requests of your partner without offending him/ her?

❏ Yes          ❏ No          ❏ Uncertain

What will you say?

41. How much personal privacy do you feel is needed?

42. I have a lack of sexual knowledge in the following areas:

43. How tense were you as you answered these questions?

44. Do you believe in counseling for sexual problems?

❏ Yes          ❏ No          ❏ Uncertain

45. Who would you feel free to talk with concerning sexual problems?

46. After reading 1 Corinthians 6:15-20 and 1 Thessalonians 4:1-8, state what you think is God's view of premarital intercourse:

47. In Hebrews 13:4 it says, "Marriage should be honored by all, and the marriage bed kept pure." I think this means:

48. After reading 1 Corinthians 7:3-5, the concept I think the writer is trying to convey is:

49. I have the following questions about sexual matters:

## Additional Resource

### *The Act of Marriage: The Beauty of Sexual Love*

by Tim and Beverly LaHaye.

This book contains valuable information on all aspects of sex from a Christian viewpoint.

> The art of mutually enjoyable lovemaking is not difficult to learn, but neither is it automatic. No one is a good lover by nature....Yet no one need settle for a lifetime of sexual frustration.

Thus Tim and Beverly LaHaye sum up this book—a most practical, thorough, and useful Christian handbook on sexual love.

# *9*
# *Sample Wedding Ceremony*

 Bill  and  Susan , you are surrounded by your family and friends, all of whom are here to share in your joy on this special occasion. It will be one of the most memorable and happy days of your lives.

On this your wedding day, you stand apart from all other beings. You stand within the beautiful circle of your love. For this reason we are here in the presence of God, to join you both in holy marriage. God has declared that marriage is an honorable and desirable state. It was designed by God to bring the ultimate in happiness and personal satisfaction. The basic guidelines are that you should put God first, the welfare of your mate second, and yourself last.

Would Mr. and Mrs.  Johnson  and Mr. and Mrs.  Wilson  please stand? It is traditional for the father of the bride to give her away. However, in a real sense, both sets of parents share in the giving and receiving. Therefore, Mr. and Mrs.  Johnson , do you not only give your son  Bill  to be  Susan's  husband, but also joyfully receive  Susan  as your daughter? (Response by parents—"We do.") Mr. and Mrs. <u>Wilson</u> do you not only joyfully give your daughter <u>Susan</u> to <u>Bill</u> as his wife, but receive <u>Bill</u> to be your son? (Response by parents—"We do.")

*Bride and groom*
*move to altar*

*Minister proceeds*  Marriage was instituted by God Himself when He said, "It is not good that man should be alone."

From the side of man God created woman to be his friend and companion...

—Not out of his head to rule over him.

—Not out of his feet to be trampled upon by him

—But out of his side to be equal with him

—And under his arm for protection

—And near his heart to be loved.

God said, "For this cause shall a man leave father and mother, and shall cleave to his wife, and the two shall be one flesh."

—One flesh in companionship

—One flesh in the control of the God-given sexual drives

—One flesh in the propagation of children

—And one flesh in the testimony of the joy of a Christian marriage.

80

*The Bible's description of true love*

The Bible tells us that true love is "slow to lose patience...love is kind...love looks for a way of being constructive. Love is not possessive...love is neither anxious to impress nor does it cherish inflated ideas of its own importance.

"Love has good manners and does not pursue selfish advantage. Love is not touchy. Love does not keep account of evil or gloat over the wickedness of other people. On the contrary, love is glad with all good men when truth prevails.

"Love knows no limit to its endurance, no end to its trust, no fading of its hope; love can outlast anything. Love is, in fact, the one thing that still stands when all else has fallen" (1 Corinthians 13).

*Admonition of Scripture to husbands and wives*

In the book of Ephesians, chapter five, marriage is likened to the mystical union of Christ and the church....

"You wives must submit to your husbands' leadership in the same way you submit to the Lord. For a husband is in charge of his wife in the same way Christ is in charge of His body the church. (He gave his very life to take care of it and be its Savior!) So you wives must willingly obey your husbands in everything, just as the church obeys Christ.

*The minister may want to make personal comments to the bride at this point*

"And you husbands, show the same kind of love to your wives as Christ showed to the church when He died for her.

"That is how husbands should treat their wives, loving them as parts of themselves. For since a man and his wife are now one, a man is really doing himself a favor and loving himself when he loves his wife! No one hates his own body but lovingly cares for it, just as Christ cares for his body the church, of which we are parts."

*The minister may want to make personal comments to the groom at this point*

"So again I say, a man must love his wife as part of himself; and the wife must see to it that she deeply respects her husband...obeying...praising and honoring him."

*Vows spoken to the minister*

After hearing the admonition of Scripture, do you _Bill_ take _Susan_ to be your lawfully wedded wife? Do you promise to support her and love her for life? Do you solemnly pledge before God and these witnesses that you will be faithful to her for the remainder of your life? If so, answer "I will." (Response by the groom)

_Susan_ do you take _Bill_ to be your lawfully wedded husband? Do you promise to love, honor, and obey him? Do you solemnly pledge before God and these witnesses that you will be his faithful wife until you are separated by death? If so, answer "I will." (Response by the bride)

*Minister will have the bride pass her flowers to her maid of honor... bride and groom will turn and face each other and will hold hands*

*Minister proceeds with personal vows*

_Bill_ please repeat after me: I love you _Susan_, and today in the presence of our families and friends, I pledge myself to you. I reaffirm my faith in Christ and dedicate our marriage to be

Christ-centered. I promise before God to love you, to honor you and cherish you. As God enables me, I will provide for all your needs and desires. Susan, I love you…be my wife.

 Susan  please repeat after me:  Bill , I love you. I've longed for this day…to be able to say publicly to our families and friends, that you are truly a man of God, a man that is tender and sensitive in his love for others. I promise to make you a home where there is peace for your soul and joy for your heart. My goal is to be a godly woman and to help fulfill our goals and dreams. I need you, and I am proud to become your wife.

*Exchange of rings*

What symbols do you offer that you will faithfully fulfill these promises? (Minister will collect the rings.)

May the circle of this ring typify your unending happiness and love, and may the triangle formed in its passing, to me, and to one another, signify that triune relationship with God who reigns above where all true marriages are made. (Minister will hand back the rings to be placed on the bride's finger and then on the groom's.)

*Bride and groom will again turn toward each other and hold hands*

*Minister proceeds*

Will you both please repeat after me: I give you this ring as a seal of my commitment and responsibility to you in the presence of these witnesses, in the name of the Father, Son, and Holy Spirit.

Since  Bill  and  Susan  have consented together in these promises and have symbolized this by the giving and receiving of these rings, I now pronounce them husband and wife. Whom God has joined together, let no man dare to separate.

*Minister will pray…couple may be standing or kneeling. They may wish to light a unity candle…after which they will again stand before the minister and face each other, holding hands*

*Ceremony of the Unity Candle*

The two outside candles of the center candelabra are lit to represent your lives to this moment. They are two distinct lights, each capable of going their separate ways. To bring bliss and happiness to your home, there must be the merging of these two lights into one light. This is what the Lord meant when He said, "On this account a man shall leave his father and mother and be joined to his wife and the two shall be one flesh."

From now on your thoughts shall be for each other rather than for your individual selves. Your plans shall be mutual, your joys and sorrows shall be shared alike.

As you each take a candle and together light the center one you will not extinguish your own candle as is usually done. Instead, place the outside candles back in their original places still lit symbolizing your individual personalities that remain, yet lives that merge together as one.

As the center candle is lit, may the radiance of this one light be a testimony of your unity in the Lord Jesus Christ.

*Bride and
groom kiss*

*Minister proceeds*   It is my pleasure now to introduce to you for the first time Mr. and Mrs. <u>Johnson</u>.

# *Wedding Checklist*

Date of wedding                     Hour

Name of church, building or home

Address

City                               Phone

## *Arranging Wedding Facilities and Services*

- ❏ Procedure for reserving the facilities
- ❏ Whether or not the church has a wedding hostess/host
- ❏ Policies concerning marrying those who have been divorced, hold differing religious views, and whether weddings are permitted on Sunday
- ❏ Policies concerning premarital counseling
- ❏ Cost, which would include use of facilities, wedding hostess/host, and janitorial clean up
- ❏ Whether or not the church has reception facilities
- ❏ Special rules or restrictions concerning photography or decorations
- ❏ Available facilities for the bridal party
- ❏ Does the church provide equipment like a kneeling bench, candle holders, or arches

❏ Permission for soloists, choir, or other special music
❏ Other

If you are planning a nontraditional wedding in a park, forest, meadow, sea or lake shore, or some other setting you will need to consider the following:

❏ Accessibility to those in your wedding party
❏ Adequate parking
❏ Privacy
❏ Will everyone be able to hear the ceremony? (Sounds do not usually carry well out of doors)
❏ Alternate plans in case of bad weather

### Clergyman or Presiding Official

Name                               Phone

Sometimes more than one clergyman or official will take part in a wedding ceremony.

Second name                        Phone

### Appointment to Discuss Wedding

Date                               Hour

Rehearsal date                     Hour

### You May Wish to Discuss:

❏ Honorarium $
❏ Use of a second clergyman or official
   Honorarium $
❏ Any special vows you may wish to incorporate
❏ Premarital counseling
   Date                    Hour
   Date                    Hour
   Date                    Hour

# Wedding Checklist

Date                         Hour
Date                         Hour
Date                         Hour

## *Wedding Hostess/Host*

Name                         Phone

Special arrangements

Honorarium $

## *Florist*

Name

Address

Phone                        Conference date

## You May Wish to Discuss:

- ❏ Bride's bouquet
- ❏ Bride's going away corsage
- ❏ Bouquets for bride's attendants
- ❏ Flowers for mothers of the bride and groom
- ❏ Flowers for grandmothers
- ❏ Boutonnieres for groom, ushers, fathers, and clergyman
- ❏ Flowers for friends and/or relatives serving at the reception
- ❏ Flowers for relatives
- ❏ Church decorations and carpet
- ❏ Reception decorations
- ❏ Time and place of delivery
- ❏ Special arrangements

## *Photographer and/or Videotaper*

Name

Address

Phone                    Conference date

**You May Wish to Discuss:**
- ❏ Types of pictures he/she takes—ask to see samples of his/her work
- ❏ The cost—get a firm price on pictures and albums
- ❏ Any special picture requests you may have
- ❏ When pictures will be taken—before, during, or after the wedding
- ❏ Expected delivery date of finished pictures
- ❏ Special arrangements

## *Caterer*

Name

Address

Phone                    Conference date

**You May Wish to Discuss:**
- ❏ Wedding cake
- ❏ Napkins
- ❏ Punch bowl
- ❏ Silver
- ❏ Beverages
- ❏ Menu

❏ If reception is out of doors, an alternate plan in case of bad weather

❏ Special arrangements

## *Music*
### Organist/pianist

Name                           Phone

Honorarium $

### Soloist

Name                           Phone

Honorarium $

### Any other special music

**Musical selections**

**Music at the reception**

Name                                    Phone

Honorarium $

**Musical selections**

## *Invitations, Announcements, and Stationery*

Number invited to ceremony:

Number invited to reception:

Number to receive announcements:

❏ Date to be mailed _____
❏ Postage
❏ Thank-you cards
❏ Printing expenses

# Wedding Checklist

❏ Name of printer

Address

Phone          Delivery date

❏ Special arrangements

## *Bridal Gown*

Shop

Date for fitting

Delivery date

Special arrangements

## *Bridesmaid Gowns*

## *Attendants and participants*

Maid of honor                                    Phone

    Dress size            Shoe            Gloves

Bridesmaid                                       Phone

    Dress size            Shoe            Gloves

Bridesmaid                                       Phone

    Dress size            Shoe            Gloves

Bridesmaid                                       Phone

    Dress size            Shoe            Gloves

Bridesmaid                                       Phone

    Dress size            Shoe            Gloves

Bridesmaid                                       Phone

    Dress size            Shoe            Gloves


Best man                                         Phone

    Tuxedo size          Shoe

Groomsman                                        Phone

    Tuxedo size          Shoe

Groomsman                                        Phone

    Tuxedo size          Shoe

Groomsman                                        Phone

    Tuxedo size          Shoe

# Wedding Checklist

Groomsman                                                 Phone

    Tuxedo size             Shoe

Groomsman                                                 Phone

    Tuxedo size             Shoe

## *Ushers*

Name                                  Phone

Name                                  Phone

Name                                  Phone

Name                                  Phone

Name                                  Phone

Name                                  Phone

## *Flower girl*

Name                                  Phone

## *Ring bearer*

Name                                  Phone

## *Candlelighters*

Name                                  Phone

Name                                  Phone

## *Guestbook attendants*

Name                                  Phone

Name                                  Phone

## *Servers at reception*

Name                                   Phone

Name                                   Phone

Name                                   Phone

Name                                   Phone

Name                                   Phone

Name                                   Phone

Name                                   Phone

Name                                   Phone

## *Janitor*

Name                                   Phone

## Special people

## *Wedding Gift List*

### Flatware Pattern

- ❏ Sterling
- ❏ Silverplate
- ❏ Stainless
- ❏ Other

Pattern                                    Registered at

Registered at

Registered at

### Dinnerware Pattern

- ❏ China
- ❏ Stoneware, earthenware
- ❏ Other

Pattern                                    Registered at

Registered at

Registered at

### Glassware Pattern:

- ❏ Crystal
- ❏ Glass

Pattern                                    Registered at

Registered at

Registered at

## Other Items That May Be Listed

- ❏ Linens
- ❏ Kitchen utensils
- ❏ Housewares and appliances
- ❏ Furniture and accessories
- ❏ Luggage
- ❏ Cleaning tools

## Miscellaneous Items Checklist

- ❏ Wedding rings—check engraving
- ❏ Marriage license
- ❏ Medical examination and blood tests
- ❏ Purchase of guest book
- ❏ Gifts for bridesmaids
- ❏ Gifts for groomsmen
- ❏ Honeymoon—reservations, tickets, car, etc.
- ❏ Newspaper announcement
- ❏ Transportation for wedding party
- ❏ Arrangements for out-of-town guests
- ❏ Appointment with hairdresser or barber
- ❏ Luggage for honeymoon
- ❏ Change Social Security card to married name
- ❏ Change drivers license to married name
- ❏ Change names on insurance policies
- ❏ Make out a will
- ❏ Open joint checking and savings accounts
- ❏ Arrange a bachelor or bachelorette party
- ❏ Arrange for after-rehearsal dinner
- ❏ "Something old, something new, something borrowed, something blue."

## Guest List

**Brides Relatives**

*Guest List*

**Groom's Relatives**

## *Guest List*

### Friends

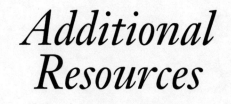

*Additional Resources*

# *Danger Signs*

## *Recognizing Caution Signals*

Marriage is a very important decision. We need to be sure we are making the right choice of a marriage partner. Anthony Florio, a professional marriage counselor, lists the following danger signs to look for:

Like red lights, blinking, danger signs mean STOP, then proceed with caution (if at all!). It is better to take this brief test before you become engaged so that if definite danger signs turn up you will have time to do something about them before committing yourself officially to marriage plans. If you are already engaged and encounter danger signs, then by all means delay your wedding plans until you can straighten out the problem areas that you or your partner have. Like icebergs, the negative traits may be hidden from you, and just the tips show what is going on beneath a supposedly mature exterior.

1. *A general uneasy feeling about the relationship. Lack of inner peace.* A nagging, aching, disturbing inside that says, "Something is wrong." Don't ignore that feeling. It may be your own temporarily numbed common sense, or it may be God's Spirit trying to communicate something to you. More than a few clients have admitted to me that they knew the marriage was a mistake even as they were walking down the aisle.

2. *Frequent arguments.* Never sure how the date will end. More fighting than fun.

3. *Avoiding discussing sensitive subjects because you're afraid of hurting your partner's feelings or starting an argument.* You find yourself thinking, "I'd better not talk about this." Perhaps subjects like: "I wish he'd show me more affection, I wish he wouldn't treat his mother so mean. I wonder why he always has a temper tantrum when he gets a flat. Can't he control it better? I wish he would shower more often."

   "She makes a pig of herself when there's a box of candy anywhere in sight—don't you suppose she cares about getting fat? I wish she'd read a book once in a while. Why can't we ever talk about something interesting instead of just superficial topics?"

4. *Getting more involved physically.* You resolve to limit the acceleration of your physical intimacy, but find that on each new date you start again at the place where you left off. Sometimes couples get involved physically as a way to avoid arguments. Just one of the reasons for this being a danger sign is that your relationship may remain on the physical level only, throughout your courtship and marriage. After you're married you may not like the personality that goes along with the body.

5. If you find yourself *always doing what your partner wants you to do.* Constantly giving in, being accommodating. This could indicate a selfish, domineering partner and/or a serious insecurity on your part.

6. *If you detect serious emotional disturbances* such as extreme fears, extreme shyness, bizarre behavior, irrational anger, inflicting physical injury, inability to demonstrate affection.

7. If you feel *you are staying in the relationship through fear.* For example, if thoughts like these go through your mind: "I wish I could get out of dating him, but I'm afraid of what he might do to me. Or he might commit suicide. I feel trapped and I couldn't stand the guilt if something happened."

8. *If your partner is constantly complaining* about apparently unreal aches and pains and going from doctor to doctor.

9. *If your partner continually makes excuses* for not finding a job. If he or she borrows money from you frequently. The partner who evades responsibility and who cannot manage his (or her) money wisely will be a poor marriage risk.

10. *If your partner is overly jealous,* suspicious, questions your word all the time, feels that everyone is against him (or her).

11. If the one you date *is a perfectionist* and *is constantly critical.* This kind of person often creates a tense unhealthy atmosphere.

12. *Treats you contemptuously.* Uses biting sarcasm.

13. *Parents and other significant people are strongly against your marriage.* Consider their reasons before you make a final decision.

14. *Lack of spiritual harmony.*

15. *Few areas of common interest.*

16. *Inability to accept constructive criticism.* Doesn't apologize when he (or she) is wrong.

## Signs That Indicate the Need for Professional Counseling

1. Undue jealousy, suspicion, distrust.

2. Constant chip-on-the-shoulder attitude.

3. Temper tantrums.

4. Unresolved anger, resentment. Vindictiveness.

5. Physically or verbally abusive.

6. Objects to or is distant to my kind of romantic involvement.

7. Severe mood swings. High elation followed by depression.

8. Constantly negative attitude. Pessimistic.

9. Suspicious of everyone. Suspects some sort of plotting against him (or her).

10. Speaks of suicide and the meaninglessness of life.[1]

---

1. From *Two to Get Ready* (Fleming H. Revell Company, 1974). Used by permission.

# *Discerning Genuine Love*

"I love to eat." "I love to swim." "I love money." "I love my dog." "I love you." What does the word *love* mean? Webster defines love as: "1. A feeling of strong personal attachment induced by sympathetic understanding, or by ties of kinship; ardent affection. 2. Tender and passionate affection for one of the opposite sex."

There are different types of love: love of things, self love, brotherly love, sexual love, and godly love. How does the love you feel for your fiancé compare with God's definition of love as found in 1 Corinthians 13?

Take this short test and compare your love and the love of your fiancé with the biblical definition of love.

Rate yourself and your fiancé on a scale of one to ten. One would be low on the love scale and ten would be high. Circle the number which you believe is descriptive of you and your fiancé at this time. For example:

*This love of which I speak is slow to lose patience.*

Myself   1   ②   3   4   5   6   7   8   9   10
Fiancé   1   2   3   4   5   6   7   8   ⑨   10

By circling two, you would be saying that you do not have a great deal of patience. On the other hand, your fiancé displays a great deal of patience as noted by circling the number nine.

1. *This love of which I speak is slow to lose patience.*

   Love doesn't demonstrate irritations or reflect anger or have a quick temper. Love bears ill-treatment from others. Love has fully accepted the character of the other individual. Love is longsuffering.

   Myself  1  2  3  4  5  6  7  8  9  10
   Fiancé  1  2  3  4  5  6  7  8  9  10

2. *Love looks for a way of being constructive.*

   Love is actively creative. Love is able to recognize needs. Love mellows all which would be harsh and austere. Love discovers successful methods of improving or contributing to the other person's life.

   Myself  1  2  3  4  5  6  7  8  9  10
   Fiancé  1  2  3  4  5  6  7  8  9  10

3. *Love is not possessive.*

   Love is not envious. Love does not hold exclusive control where one is allowed little or no freedom to fulfill him- or herself apart from the other individual. Love does not boil over with jealousy.

   Myself  1  2  3  4  5  6  7  8  9  10
   Fiancé  1  2  3  4  5  6  7  8  9  10

4. *Love is not anxious to impress.*

   Love does not brag. Love doesn't seek to make an impression or create an image for personal gain. Love does not show itself off. Love is not ostentatious. Love does not make a parade.

   Myself  1  2  3  4  5  6  7  8  9  10
   Fiancé  1  2  3  4  5  6  7  8  9  10

5. *Love doesn't cherish inflated ideas of its own importance.*

Love does not put on airs. Love is not self-centered. Love has the ability to change and to accept change. Love is flexible. Love is not conceited, arrogant, or inflated with pride. Love doesn't allow or accept the idea that life revolves around itself. Love is not on an ego trip.

Myself  1  2  3  4  5  6  7  8  9  10
Fiancé  1  2  3  4  5  6  7  8  9  10

6. *Love has good manners.*

Love has respect for others which results in a set of Christ-centered standards. Love does not act unbecomingly or unmannerly. Love has discretion and knows what is proper and when. Love is not indecent.

Myself  1  2  3  4  5  6  7  8  9  10
Fiancé  1  2  3  4  5  6  7  8  9  10

7. *Love does not pursue selfish advantage.*

Love does not insist on its own way. Love does not have primary concern for personal sexual appetites or social status but concern for needs of the other person and other family members. Love does not pursue selfish aims.

Myself  1  2  3  4  5  6  7  8  9  10
Fiancé  1  2  3  4  5  6  7  8  9  10

8. *Love is not touchy.*

Love is not easily angered. Love is not hypersensitive or easily hurt. Love does not take things too personally. Love is thick-skinned. Love is not emotionally involved with personal opinions so that to reject ideas is to reject the one giving them. Love bears no malice. Love is not irritable or resentful.

Myself  1  2  3  4  5  6  7  8  9  10
Fiancé  1  2  3  4  5  6  7  8  9  10

9. *Love does not keep account of evil.*

Love doesn't review wrongs that have been forgiven. Love doesn't dwell on past evil. Love keeps no score of past hurts. Love destroys evidence of past mistakes when possible.

Myself  1  2  3  4  5  6  7  8  9  10
Fiancé  1  2  3  4  5  6  7  8  9  10

10. *Love does not gloat over the wickedness of other people.*

Love doesn't compare self with others for self-justification. Love doesn't use other's evil to excuse personal weakness. Love doesn't say, "Everyone's doing it." Love does not rejoice at injustice and unrighteousness.

Myself  1  2  3  4  5  6  7  8  9  10
Fiancé  1  2  3  4  5  6  7  8  9  10

11. *On the contrary, love is glad with all godly people when truth prevails.*

Love is active in fellowship with dedicated Christians. Love is occupied with spiritual objectives. Love rejoices at the victory of truth.

Myself  1  2  3  4  5  6  7  8  9  10
Fiancé  1  2  3  4  5  6  7  8  9  10

12. *Love knows no limit to its forbearance.*

Love has the ability to live with the inconsistencies of others. Love is slow to expose. Love can overlook faults. Love has empathy for the problems of others. Love can endure many hardships.

Myself  1  2  3  4  5  6  7  8  9  10
Fiancé  1  2  3  4  5  6  7  8  9  10

13. *Love knows no end to its trust.*

Love expresses faith in everything. Love believes in the person and the person's worth without question. Love is eager to believe the best and has no reason to doubt the other person's integrity.

Myself  1  2  3  4  5  6  7  8  9  10
Fiancé  1  2  3  4  5  6  7  8  9  10

14. *Love knows no fading of its hope.*

Love is not fickle. Love has perfect peace and confidence that God is primarily responsible for introducing the right partner at the right time. Love is positive and not negative.

Myself  1  2  3  4  5  6  7  8  9  10
Fiancé  1  2  3  4  5  6  7  8  9  10

15. *Love has unlimited endurance.*

Love is able to outlast anything. Love is able to endure all obstacles and even love in the face of unreturned love. Love does not lose heart but has perseverance. There is nothing that love cannot face.

Myself  1  2  3  4  5  6  7  8  9  10
Fiancé  1  2  3  4  5  6  7  8  9  10

If you love someone you will be loyal no matter what the cost. You will always believe in that person, always expect the best, and always stand your ground in defending him or her.

Love is the one thing that still stands when all else has fallen. In this life we have three great lasting qualities…Faith, Hope, and Love. But the greatest of them is Love.

Love is not just a feeling but a commitment of the person and his or her will. Love is a decision to love an imperfect person.

# 13 *Descriptive Characteristics*

Place an X by each word which you *honestly believe* is descriptive of you or your fiancé. Then discuss your findings with each other. Explain the reason why you chose a particular word.

|  |  | Myself | My fiancé |
|---|---|:---:|:---:|
| 1. | Persuasive | ❏ | ❏ |
| 2. | Wonderful | ❏ | ❏ |
| 3. | Peaceful | ❏ | ❏ |
| 4. | Enthusiastic | ❏ | ❏ |
| 5. | Boisterous | ❏ | ❏ |
| 6. | Soothing | ❏ | ❏ |
| 7. | Magnetic | ❏ | ❏ |
| 8. | Forceful | ❏ | ❏ |
| 9. | Friendly | ❏ | ❏ |
| 10. | Unselfish | ❏ | ❏ |
| 11. | Timid | ❏ | ❏ |
| 12. | Tolerant | ❏ | ❏ |
| 13. | Brave | ❏ | ❏ |
| 14. | Slow | ❏ | ❏ |
| 15. | Proud | ❏ | ❏ |

|  |  | Myself | My fiancé |
|---|---|:---:|:---:|
| 16. | Exciting | ❏ | ❏ |
| 17. | Attractive | ❏ | ❏ |
| 18. | Deliberate | ❏ | ❏ |
| 19. | Confident | ❏ | ❏ |
| 20. | Open-minded | ❏ | ❏ |
| 21. | Generous | ❏ | ❏ |
| 22. | Bitter | ❏ | ❏ |
| 23. | Calm | ❏ | ❏ |
| 24. | Outgoing | ❏ | ❏ |
| 25. | Shy | ❏ | ❏ |
| 26. | Patient | ❏ | ❏ |
| 27. | Self-motivated | ❏ | ❏ |
| 28. | Compassionate | ❏ | ❏ |
| 29. | Talented | ❏ | ❏ |
| 30. | Kind | ❏ | ❏ |
| 31. | Ambitious | ❏ | ❏ |
| 32. | Softhearted | ❏ | ❏ |
| 33. | Gifted | ❏ | ❏ |
| 34. | Egotist | ❏ | ❏ |
| 35. | High-spirited | ❏ | ❏ |
| 36. | Happy | ❏ | ❏ |
| 37. | Humble | ❏ | ❏ |
| 38. | Undisciplined | ❏ | ❏ |
| 39. | Shallow | ❏ | ❏ |
| 40. | Spiritually mature | ❏ | ❏ |
| 41. | Bad mouth | ❏ | ❏ |
| 42. | Suspicious | ❏ | ❏ |
| 43. | Overbearing | ❏ | ❏ |
| 44. | Touchy | ❏ | ❏ |
| 45. | Jealous | ❏ | ❏ |
| 46. | Gossip | ❏ | ❏ |
| 47. | Nervy | ❏ | ❏ |

# Descriptive Characteristics

|  |  | Myself | My fiancé |
|---|---|---|---|
| 48. | Magnificent | ❑ | ❑ |
| 49. | Stubborn | ❑ | ❑ |
| 50. | Big-hearted | ❑ | ❑ |
| 51. | Cautious | ❑ | ❑ |
| 52. | Stimulating | ❑ | ❑ |
| 53. | Afraid | ❑ | ❑ |
| 54. | Outspoken | ❑ | ❑ |
| 55. | Helpful | ❑ | ❑ |
| 56. | Materialistic | ❑ | ❑ |
| 57. | Unhealthy | ❑ | ❑ |
| 58. | Insensitive | ❑ | ❑ |
| 59. | Gentle | ❑ | ❑ |
| 60. | Humorous | ❑ | ❑ |
| 61. | Unattractive | ❑ | ❑ |
| 62. | Competent | ❑ | ❑ |
| 63. | Daring | ❑ | ❑ |
| 64. | Religious | ❑ | ❑ |
| 65. | Dynamic | ❑ | ❑ |
| 66. | Well-mannered | ❑ | ❑ |
| 67. | Superior | ❑ | ❑ |
| 68. | Stern | ❑ | ❑ |
| 69. | Venturesome | ❑ | ❑ |
| 70. | Faithful | ❑ | ❑ |
| 71. | Conceited | ❑ | ❑ |
| 72. | Selfish | ❑ | ❑ |
| 73. | Polite | ❑ | ❑ |
| 74. | Eager | ❑ | ❑ |
| 75. | Hostile | ❑ | ❑ |
| 76. | Aggressive | ❑ | ❑ |
| 77. | Disrespectful | ❑ | ❑ |
| 78. | Wishy-washy | ❑ | ❑ |
| 79. | Dishonest | ❑ | ❑ |

|  |  | Myself | My fiancé |
|---|---|---|---|
| 80. | Moody | ❑ | ❑ |
| 81. | Dependable | ❑ | ❑ |
| 82. | Overly competitive | ❑ | ❑ |
| 83. | Talkative | ❑ | ❑ |
| 84. | Weak-willed | ❑ | ❑ |
| 85. | Personable | ❑ | ❑ |
| 86. | Strong-willed | ❑ | ❑ |
| 87. | Angry | ❑ | ❑ |
| 88. | Productive | ❑ | ❑ |
| 89. | Negative | ❑ | ❑ |
| 90. | Idealistic | ❑ | ❑ |
| 91. | Impractical | ❑ | ❑ |
| 92. | Easy-going | ❑ | ❑ |
| 93. | Stingy | ❑ | ❑ |
| 94. | Conservative | ❑ | ❑ |
| 95. | Loud | ❑ | ❑ |
| 96. | Independent | ❑ | ❑ |
| 97. | Sarcastic | ❑ | ❑ |
| 98. | Decisive | ❑ | ❑ |
| 99. | Self-sufficient | ❑ | ❑ |
| 100. | Analytical | ❑ | ❑ |
| 101. | Theoretical | ❑ | ❑ |
| 102. | Loyal | ❑ | ❑ |
| 103. | Unsociable | ❑ | ❑ |
| 104. | Apprehensive | ❑ | ❑ |
| 105. | Diplomatic | ❑ | ❑ |
| 106. | Unmotivated | ❑ | ❑ |
| 107. | Restless | ❑ | ❑ |
| 108. | Exaggerates | ❑ | ❑ |
| 109. | Optimistic | ❑ | ❑ |
| 110. | Domineering | ❑ | ❑ |
| 111. | Leader | ❑ | ❑ |

# Descriptive Characteristics

| | | Myself | My fiancé |
|---|---|---|---|
| 112. | Unemotional | ❏ | ❏ |
| 113. | Sensitive | ❏ | ❏ |
| 114. | Self-sacrificing | ❏ | ❏ |
| 115. | Critical | ❏ | ❏ |
| 116. | Indecisive | ❏ | ❏ |
| 117. | Warm | ❏ | ❏ |
| 118. | Undependable | ❏ | ❏ |
| 119. | Carefree | ❏ | ❏ |
| 120. | Fearful | ❏ | ❏ |
| 121. | Practical | ❏ | ❏ |
| 122. | Inconsiderate | ❏ | ❏ |
| 123. | Crafty | ❏ | ❏ |
| 124. | Perfectionist | ❏ | ❏ |
| 125. | Rigid | ❏ | ❏ |
| 126. | Revengeful | ❏ | ❏ |
| 127. | Efficient | ❏ | ❏ |
| 128. | Spectator | ❏ | ❏ |
| 129. | Sensible | ❏ | ❏ |
| 130. | Self-protective | ❏ | ❏ |

# *Insight Questions*

Please complete the following sentences. From your answers you will gain new insights into your thoughts and feelings.*

1. When I hear from others that you have complained about me, I:

2. When some other interest seems more important to you than I do, I:

---

* These insight questions are reprinted from John Powell, *The Secret of Staying in Love* (Niles, IL: Argus Communications). Used by permission.

3. When you seem to hold back something from me, I:

4. When I hold back something from you, I:

5. When you look at other men/women with obvious interest, I:

6. When you are late and I have to wait for you, I:

7. When you have a strong interest which I cannot share, I:

8.  When I try to convince you of something and you can't accept it, I:

9.  When you seem to be rejecting my feelings, I:

10. When you praise or compliment me, I:

11. When I am confronted with or think of that which I fear most, I:

12. When I think you are judging me, I:

13. When you become angry with me, I:

14. When I have to admit that I am wrong, I:

15. When I think you are taking a superior role in our dialogues and discussions, I:

16. When I do not seem able to reach you, I:

17. When you frown at me, I:

18. When you are being too hard on yourself, I:

19. When you smile at me, I:

20. When you reach out and touch me, I:

21. When I think of praying with you, I:

22. When you make a sacrifice for me, I:

23. When others notice our closeness, I:

24. When we appear as a partnership, not as individuals only, I:

25. When I reflect that you love me, I:

26. When you seem annoyed with me, I:

27. When I have the opportunity to be alone and enjoy some solitude, I:

28. When we have been separated a long time, I:

29. When I reflect that we are growing in mutual knowledge, I:

30. When we are holding hands, I:

31. When we are making plans together, I:

32. When I am buying you a gift, I:

33. When I reach out and touch you, I:

34. When you interrupt me in conversation, I:

35. When we are in some form of competition like cards or an athletic contest, I:

36. When you say no to one of my requests, I:

37. When I think I have hurt your feelings, I:

38.  When you apologize to me, I:

39.  When we can spend a quiet evening together, I:

40.  When you help me locate my feelings, I:

41.  When I hear from others that you have bragged about me, I:

42.  When others look at you with obvious interest, I:

43.  When you cry, I:

44.  When you are sick, I:

45.  When I think about your death and what life would be without you, I:

46.  When we hear "our song," I:

47.  When you ask me to help you, I:

48.  When I have to apologize to you, I:

49. When you surprise me with something nice, I:

50. When you seem to appreciate me, I:

51. When you laugh at my jokes, I:

52. When I think you are not recognizing my needs, I:

53. When I make a mistake and you point it out, I:

54. When you are holding me in your arms, I:

55. When our routines are different and our interests separate us, I:

56. When I am late and you have to wait for me, I:

57. When I reach out to touch you, I:

58. When I think you don't believe me, I:

# 15 Decisions in Marriage

There are many decisions that have to be made in a marriage. Some are made by the husband, some are made by the wife, and some are shared equally. Read over the following list of decisions and indicate who you feel should make the decision (H for husbands...W for wives...B for both), then write down why. Compare and discuss your responses with the answers of your fiancé.

1. Who decides on formal or informal engagement?

2. Who decides date of wedding?

3. Who decides what type of wedding?

4. Who decides whether to have a honeymoon?

5. Who decides where to go on a honeymoon?

6. Who decides where to live?

7. Who decides when to move?

8. Who decides whether the wife should work?

9. Who decides whether the wife should give up her job when a child is born?

10. Who makes financial decisions?

11. Who decides if incomes are to be shared?

12. Who decides who will handle the checkbook?

13. Who decides about borrowing money and going into debt?

14. Who decides on the budget?

15. Who makes justified complaints to tradespeople?

16. Who decides to buy a car?

17. Whose name is the car in?

18. Who looks after the car?

19. Who decides which house to buy?

20. Whose name is it in?

21. Who decides on the interior decor?

22. Who decides on the exterior decor?

23. Who decides on the furnishings?

24. Who decides on the landscaping?

25. Who takes care of the yard work?

26. Who is responsible for life and health insurance?

27. Who makes retirement plans?

28. Who decides activities after retirement?

29. Who takes the active role in sex?

30. Who decides whether to have children?

31. Who takes responsibility for contraception?

32. Who decides when to have children?

33. Who decides how many children to have?

34. Who takes responsibility for the education of the children?

35. Who helps the children with homework?

36. Who takes responsibilities in emergencies?

37. Who decides political issues for the family?

38. Who decides how to raise the children?

39. Who decides which friends to socialize with?

40. Who invites people to the house?

41. Who chooses television programs?

42. Whose food tastes prevail?

43. Who plans the day-to-day meals?

44. Who does the grocery shopping for the family?

45. Who decides when to go out?

46. Who decides where to go out?

47. Who decides what to do and where to go on vacations?

48. What relatives do you keep in touch with?

49. Whose job is it to keep in touch with the relatives?

50. Who remembers anniversaries and birthdays?

51. Who copes with family disasters?

52. Who decides whether to go to church or not?

53. Who decides which church to go to?

# Other Good
# Harvest House Reading

**BEFORE YOU SAY I DO**
by *Norman Wright*

With over 500,000 copies sold, this guide is now updated for the '90s. Couples will explore how to clarify role expectations, establish a healthy sexual relationship, handle finances, and acquire a solid understanding of how to develop a biblical relationship.

**AFTER YOU SAY I DO**
by *Norman Wright*

Couples will find a wealth of practical ideas for enriching their future together. Includes how to resolve conflict in marriage, setting goals, handling finances, and building healthy in-law relationships.

**WHAT TO DO UNTIL LOVE FINDS YOU**
by *Michelle McKinney-Hammond*
Drawing from 16 years of being single and counseling single women, McKinney-Hammond offers women practical, godly advice on how to handle sexual temptations regardless of past experience, develop internal and external beauty, and wait joyfully for God's timing.

**FINDING YOUR PERFECT MATE**
by *Norman Wright*

Thoughtful words of wisdom and encouragement on one of life's most important turning points. Dynamic insights based on years of premarital counseling for people who seek God's guidance in finding a perfect lifetime companion.

# Other Books
# by Bob Phillips